LOUVRE MUSEUM

TRAVEL GUIDE
2024-2025

Master the Art of Visiting: Strategies to Explore the World's Most Iconic Museum

D1736293

PAUL R. BAKER

1

TABLE OF CONTENT

Foreword 9

A Personal Invitation to Explore the Louvre 9

Embracing the Louvre: More than a Museum 12

How to Use This Guide 13

Frequently Asked Questions About the Louvre 15

Chapter 1: Planning Your Visit 21

Best Times to Visit the Louvre 21

Tickets and Tours: Choosing Your Ideal Experience....22

Navigating the Arrondissements: Getting to the Louvre
....25

Lodging: Stay Close to the Action...........................27

Chapter 2: History Unveiled 31

The Origins of the Louvre: From Fortress to Art Haven
....31

Significant Milestones in Louvre History....................33

The Louvre During War and Peace 36

Chapter 3: Masterpieces of the Louvre 39

Must-See Treasures: Mona Lisa and Beyond...............39

Hidden Gems: Lesser-Known Wonders 42

Thematic Exploration of the Louvre: A Journey Through Time 44

Chapter 4: Thematic Tours Inside the Louvre 49

The Romantic's Path: Love and Mystery in Art...........49

The Connoisseur's Route: Masterpieces and their Masters...52

Family Friendly: Engaging the Young Art Lover 55

Chapter 5: Architectural Wonders 59

Palatial Splendors: The Louvre as a Royal Residence ..59

Modern Additions: The Pyramid and Contemporary Flares..62

Sculptures and Gardens: Art Beyond the Walls 65

Chapter 6: Cultural Immersion 69

Art Workshops and Lectures: Learn from Experts........69

Photographic Opportunities: Capturing Timeless Moments 71

Night at the Museum: Evening Events and Special Tours 75

3

Chapter 7: Dining and Shopping 79

Culinary Arts: Best Eateries Within and Near the Louvre

.... 79

Souvenirs and Artifacts: Shopping with Sophistication 82

Chapter 8: Tips and Tricks for the Savvy Traveler 85

Avoiding the Crowds: Insider Secrets 85

The Art of Appreciation: Enhancing Your Viewing

Experience 87

Accessibility and Assistance: Ensuring a Smooth Visit 89

Chapter 9: Beyond the Louvre 93

Parisian Art Scene: Other Must-Visit Locations 93

Day Trips Worth the Detour 96

Chapter 10: Recommended Itineraries 99

The Express Tour: Louvre Highlights in 2 Hours 99

A Full-Day Immersion: Masterpieces and Hidden

Treasures 101

Family Fun: Engaging the Kids with a Half-Day Tour

.... 103

Themed Tour: Love and Mythology in Art (Half-Day) 106

Chapter 11: Practical Information.................................109

Opening Hours and Admission...................................109

Visitor Services...111

Safety and Security 112

Helpful Tips for a Stress-Free Visit............................115

Language Tips and Phrases for Visiting the Louvre ...116

Chapter 12: Essential Travel Checklist 121

Final Thoughts 127

LOUVRE MUSEUM

LOUVRE MUSEUM

MAP OF LOUVRE MUSEUM

Saint-Denis

Louvre Museum
Landmark art museum
with vast collection
Recently viewed

Disneyland F

illes

A15

A1

A104

A86

A4

N104

A6a
A6B

N118   A10   A6

N6

D471

SCAN THE QR CODE

FOREWORD

A Personal Invitation to Explore the Louvre

Have you ever wondered what it feels like to stand in front of a piece of art that has shaped the course of history? The Louvre offers that moment—thousands of times over.

I still remember my first visit, stepping into the Louvre with wide eyes and a heart full of excitement. The museum was more than I imagined—each room a portal to different times, places, and lives. It wasn't just about the art, but about the stories that each masterpiece told. Every piece felt like an invitation to step closer and understand the emotions, struggles, and triumphs of those who created them.

The Louvre isn't just a museum—it's a living, breathing experience. Whether you're exploring the elegance of ancient civilizations or standing in awe of Renaissance genius, every corner of the museum resonates with the weight of history. It's a place where the world's greatest works come together, not just to be admired, but to be felt.

You'll find that it's not just about what you see, but how each piece draws you in and leaves an imprint on your own story.

What makes the Louvre so special is its ability to overwhelm you in the best way possible. With over 35,000 pieces spread across miles of galleries, it can feel like you're diving into an ocean of art and culture. From the gleaming glass pyramid to the quiet halls housing timeless masterpieces, the Louvre offers moments of both grandeur and intimate discovery. Whether you're standing before the mystery of the Mona Lisa or pausing to take in the quiet power of the Winged Victory, every moment here has something to offer.

Visiting the Louvre in 2024-2025 presents an opportunity like no other. Recent upgrades in the museum's layout and displays have made it more accessible and visually engaging, giving visitors an improved experience. Special exhibitions are featuring rare pieces not seen in years, allowing you to view the museum's collection from a new angle.

The Louvre is also introducing new interactive tools that enhance your experience, from digital guides to augmented reality features. These additions provide a modern way to explore the museum while still enjoying its traditional beauty.

With global travel conditions continuing to improve, the timing is perfect for a visit. The Louvre is welcoming visitors in a way that allows for a more thoughtful and less crowded exploration, making 2024-2025 an ideal time to truly enjoy the museum's vast collection at your own pace.

This guide goes beyond just listing what to see at the Louvre—it's crafted to make your visit unforgettable and purposeful. With detailed, easy-to-follow advice, it helps you explore the museum with confidence, offering practical strategies and insider tips that most other guides overlook. Whether you're visiting for the first time or returning to explore new corners, this guide ensures you'll see the best of the Louvre without feeling lost or overwhelmed.

Unlike many guides that simply scratch the surface, this one dives deeper.

You'll gain a fresh perspective on the artworks, understanding not just their historical context but also their emotional impact. Each section is designed to help you connect with the art in a way that's personal, giving your visit meaning and depth. Let's start this journey together— your adventure at the Louvre is about to begin.

Embracing the Louvre: More than a Museum

The Louvre isn't just a place where art is displayed—it's a monument that has witnessed centuries of change, growth, and evolution. As you walk through its halls, you're stepping into a living narrative that stretches from the medieval fortress it once was to the world-renowned museum it is today. Every corner of the Louvre holds the spirit of the eras it has passed through, reflecting not only the history of France but of the world itself. It's this deep connection to history that makes the Louvre more than just a collection of art—it's a cultural icon that tells the story of humanity.

Visiting the Louvre isn't simply about looking at paintings and sculptures; it's about experiencing something larger than yourself. Each room invites you to engage, not just with your eyes, but with your mind and heart.

As you move from one gallery to the next, you'll find yourself reflecting on the deeper meanings behind the works, making connections to your own experiences and emotions. It's an intellectual and emotional journey, one that stays with you long after you've left.

Despite its grand scale, the Louvre offers moments of personal connection. Amidst the thousands of works on display, each piece tells its own story, creating a sense of intimacy even in such a vast space. Whether it's a quiet corner with a lesser-known painting or the detailed brushstrokes of a world-famous masterpiece, each visit feels uniquely personal. No two people will experience the Louvre in the same way, and that's part of its magic—each visit is a chance to see something new, to discover a piece of art that resonates with you on a personal level.

How to Use This Guide

This guide is designed to be your companion before, during, and even after your visit to the Louvre, offering practical insights and expert advice along the way. To make the most of your experience, here's how you can navigate the guide efficiently and tailor it to your needs:

The guide is divided into chapters that cover different aspects of the Louvre, from its history to the must-see collections, to hidden gems that often go unnoticed.

Each chapter is structured to be easy to reference, whether you're preparing for your visit, exploring the museum, or reflecting afterward. You can quickly jump between sections depending on what you're looking for at any given moment—whether it's the layout of the museum, insider tips, or advice on how to spend your time wisely.

To personalize your visit, think about what interests you most. Are you a solo traveler looking for a quiet, reflective experience? Or are you visiting with family, trying to keep everyone engaged? This guide offers suggestions for different types of visitors, with tips on how to adjust your itinerary based on time constraints, personal preferences, or group dynamics. Whether you have just a few hours or an entire day, you'll find tailored advice to help you make the most of your time.

Consider marking or highlighting key sections of the guide that stand out to you.

You might find a thematic tour that interests you, an insider tip about an overlooked section of the museum, or a recommendation for a nearby café that's perfect for a break.

Having these sections ready will save you time and make your visit smoother, allowing you to focus on enjoying the Louvre rather than scrambling for information on the go.

Frequently Asked Questions About the Louvre

1. What are the Louvre's opening hours?

The Louvre operates every day except Tuesday. Standard hours are 9 AM to 6 PM. On Wednesdays and Fridays, the museum stays open until 9:45 PM for evening visitors.

2. How much does it cost to visit the Louvre?

Tickets purchased online cost €17, while buying them on-site is €15. Admission is free for visitors under 18, residents of the European Economic Area aged 18-25, and select other groups on certain days.

3. Can I skip the lines at the Louvre?

Yes, purchasing tickets online or through the official app allows you to skip the main ticket line and enter faster.

4. When is the best time to visit to avoid large crowds?

To avoid peak crowds, it's best to visit early in the morning, shortly after the museum opens, or in the late afternoon on weekdays. Visiting during extended hours on Wednesdays or Fridays is also a good option for fewer crowds.

5. Can I take pictures inside the Louvre?

Photography without flash is permitted in most areas. However, in some special exhibitions, photos may not be allowed, and signs will indicate any restrictions. Always respect the rules to protect the artwork.

6. How long does it take to explore the Louvre?

The museum is vast, and it could take a full day or more to see everything. If you're short on time, you can cover the highlights like the Mona Lisa and the Venus de Milo in about 2-3 hours. For a more in-depth experience, allow for several hours or multiple visits.

7. What's the best way to navigate such a large museum?

Given the Louvre's size, using a map or the official Louvre app is highly recommended. These tools help you locate key exhibits and organize your visit.

Planning ahead for the sections or artworks you want to see most will save time and energy.

8. Does the Louvre offer guided tours?

Yes, guided tours are available through the museum, offering both group and private options.

These tours are a great way to gain deeper insights into specific collections or themes.

9. Are there places to eat within the Louvre?

Yes, there are several cafés and restaurants inside the Louvre, where you can take a break and enjoy a meal or snack. Popular spots include Café Richelieu and Café Marly.

10. Is the Louvre accessible for visitors with disabilities?

The Louvre provides accessible facilities, including ramps, elevators, and wheelchairs, which are available for free. The museum also offers tours and services designed for visitors with visual or hearing impairments.

11. Is there a specific dress code for visiting the Louvre?

There's no formal dress code, but it's a good idea to wear comfortable shoes as the museum requires a lot of walking.

Many visitors prefer smart-casual attire to complement the setting, though casual clothes are also fine.

12. What's the easiest way to reach the Louvre using public transportation?

The Paris Métro is the most convenient way to reach the Louvre.

Take Line 1 or Line 7 and get off at Palais Royal–Musée du Louvre. Several bus lines, including 21, 69, and 72, also stop nearby.

13. Is there a place to store bags or coats?

Yes, the Louvre offers a free cloakroom where you can store coats, small bags, and umbrellas. Keep in mind that large luggage and oversized items are not allowed inside the museum.

14. Can I leave and re-enter the museum on the same day with one ticket?

No, re-entry is not permitted after leaving the Louvre. Be sure to see everything you want before you exit.

15. Are children allowed at the Louvre, and are there activities for them?

Children are welcome at the Louvre, and the museum offers special activities, tours, and workshops designed for younger visitors to make their experience more enjoyable.

Chapter 1: Planning Your Visit

Best Times to Visit the Louvre

Choosing the right time to visit the Louvre can greatly enhance your experience by minimizing waits and maximizing your enjoyment of the art. Here are some suggestions on when to plan your visit:

Optimal Months and Seasons: The quieter months, from November through February, are ideal if you prefer to avoid large crowds. The museum is less busy, allowing for a more personal connection with the artworks. For those who appreciate milder weather and don't mind a few more visitors, spring offers a pleasant balance, making it a great time to explore both the museum and its surroundings.

Best Times of Day: Visiting early in the morning or later in the afternoon can make your experience much more enjoyable. The museum opens its doors at 9 AM, and during the first hour, the galleries are notably quieter. Alternatively, consider a late afternoon visit, especially on Wednesdays and Fridays, when the museum remains open until 9:45 PM. These times allow you to enjoy the Louvre in a more tranquil setting.

Extended Hours: Wednesday and Friday evenings are special at the Louvre, with extended opening hours until 9:45 PM. These evenings offer a different atmosphere, quieter and more serene, which many find more conducive to appreciating the art. It's a perfect opportunity to see the Louvre in a new light, literally and figuratively.

Visiting on Free Days and Holidays: The Louvre offers free admission on the first Saturday of each month from 6 PM to 9:45 PM and on Bastille Day (July 14). While these days can provide significant savings, they also attract larger crowds. If you choose to visit on these days, it's wise to arrive early or during typically less crowded times, like late evening, to make the most of your visit.

Tickets and Tours: Choosing Your Ideal Experience

Selecting the right ticket and tour options can significantly enhance your visit to the Louvre. Here's a guide to help you choose the best experience tailored to your interests and schedule:

Ticket Options:

- **General Admission**: This ticket grants access to the museum's permanent collection and temporary exhibitions. It's ideal for visitors who prefer to explore at their own pace.

- **Skip-the-Line Passes**: If your time is limited or you prefer not to wait, consider a skip-the-line ticket. These passes allow you to bypass the often lengthy queues, offering a more streamlined entry.

Guided Tours:

- **Thematic Tours**: These are perfect for visitors with specific interests in art or history. Thematic tours focus on particular styles, periods, or collections within the Louvre.

- **Private Tours**: For a more personalized experience, private tours offer one-on-one interaction with knowledgeable guides. This option is excellent for those who wish to delve deeper into the art and history of the Louvre.

- **Family-Friendly Tours**: Designed to engage children and adults alike, these tours make art appreciation accessible and enjoyable for younger visitors.

Booking Tickets:

- To make the most of your visit, book your tickets online in advance. This not only saves you time by avoiding long lines but also ensures you won't miss out due to sold-out days, especially during peak seasons.

Special Access Tours:

- **VIP Tours**: These tours offer experiences such as early entry before the museum opens to the public or private viewings of famous works. If you're seeking exclusivity and a deeper connection with the art, a VIP tour may be the ideal choice.

Navigating the Arrondissements: Getting to the Louvre

Arriving at the Louvre can be as much a part of your Paris adventure as exploring the museum itself. Whether you're using public transportation, walking, or driving, here's how to navigate to the Louvre with ease:

Using the Paris Metro:

- The most convenient metro lines for reaching the Louvre are Line 1 and Line 7. For Line 1, alight at the Palais Royal-Musée du Louvre station; for Line 7, exit at Pyramides. Both stops are a short walk to the museum's main entrance. The metro is efficient and can save you time, especially during busy traffic hours.

Walking Routes:

- If you're staying in central Paris, consider a scenic walk to the Louvre. From neighborhoods like Le Marais or Saint-Germain-des-Prés, you can enjoy a leisurely stroll through some of Paris's charming streets.

- These routes not only offer a glimpse into Parisian life but also pass by several notable landmarks and cafes where you can pause and soak in the city's vibrant atmosphere.

Cycling or Driving:

- Paris is cyclist-friendly, with numerous bike rental options available, including the popular Vélib' bike-sharing service. If you prefer to drive, be aware that parking in the area can be challenging. The Carrousel du Louvre and the Saint-Germain l'Auxerrois are among the nearest parking facilities, though spaces might be limited during peak hours.

Accessibility:

- The Louvre is committed to accessibility for all visitors. If you or someone you're traveling with requires assistance, use the Pyramid entrance, which is equipped with elevators and ramps to accommodate wheelchairs.

- Additionally, all major metro stations near the Louvre are equipped with elevators and clear signage, making them accessible for visitors with mobility challenges.

Lodging: Stay Close to the Action

Choosing the right accommodations can greatly enhance your visit to the Louvre and your overall experience in Paris. Here's a guide to help you select the best lodging options that fit your preferences and budget:

Luxury Hotels:

- For those seeking the epitome of comfort and convenience, there are several luxury hotels within walking distance of the Louvre. Consider the Le Meurice, located directly across from the Tuileries Garden, which combines opulent décor with impeccable service. Another superb choice is the Hôtel de Crillon, which offers stunning views and world-class amenities, ensuring your stay is as memorable as your visit to the museum.

Mid-Range and Boutique Hotels:

- If you're looking for good value without sacrificing location, there are numerous mid-range hotels and boutique accommodations nearby.

- The Hotel Montpensier offers a comfortable stay with easy access to the museum at a more affordable price point. Boutique hotels like the Drawing Hotel feature unique artistic décor and a cozy atmosphere, providing a charming retreat after a day of sightseeing.

Unique Stays:

- For a more authentic Parisian experience, consider renting an Airbnb apartment or staying in a historic guesthouse. These accommodations often offer more space and the opportunity to live like a local. Options in the Marais or the Latin Quarter provide a picturesque backdrop to your stay, with easy access to both the Louvre and vibrant local cafes, markets, and shops.

Booking Tips:

- To get the best deals, book your accommodations several months in advance, especially if you plan to visit during peak tourist seasons like spring and summer. Keep an eye out for special promotions or discounts during the less busy months, such as late fall and winter. Websites like Booking.com or Expedia often feature competitive rates and can help you secure a great deal.

CHAPTER 2: HISTORY UNVEILED

The Origins of the Louvre: From Fortress to Art Haven

Early Beginnings as a Fortress:

The Louvre's history began in the 12th century when King Philip II constructed it as a fortress to defend Paris against Viking raids along the Seine. Initially, the Louvre was a formidable structure with a moat and high walls, strategically designed for protection and surveillance. This origin story sets the stage for the building's remarkable transition over the centuries.

Royal Residence and Architectural Evolution:

- Over the years, the Louvre underwent significant modifications. Under Charles V and later, Francis I, the fortress transformed into a luxurious royal residence.

These monarchs expanded and enhanced the structure, incorporating elements that reflected the Renaissance aesthetics prevalent at the time. Each modification served not only practical purposes but also symbolized the growing influence and affluence of French royalty.

Foundation of the Art Collection:

- Francis I's passion for the arts radically changed the Louvre's purpose. His acquisitions of masterpieces like Leonardo da Vinci's *Mona Lisa* laid the groundwork for the Louvre's future as an art museum. This marked the beginning of the collection that would eventually become central to French culture and identity, showcasing not just European but eventually global artistry.

Transition to a Public Museum:

- The most transformative period for the Louvre came during the French Revolution, when it was established as a public museum in 1793.

This shift was not just architectural but ideological, reflecting the revolutionary ideals of liberty, equality, and fraternity. Opening the royal collection to the public signified a dramatic shift from royal privilege to public right, making art accessible to everyone and turning the Louvre into a symbol of national pride and cultural heritage.

Significant Milestones in Louvre History

The Louvre's journey to becoming the world's most iconic museum is marked by pivotal events that have shaped its structure, collections, and global standing. Here, we explore key moments that highlight this transformation.

Establishment as a Public Museum:

- The Louvre was officially opened to the public in 1793, during the tumultuous times of the French Revolution. This was a groundbreaking moment, as it transformed what was once a royal palace into a museum, making a vast collection of art accessible to the public.

This decision reflected the revolutionary ideals of breaking down the barriers between the ruling classes and the public, and it marked the beginning of the Louvre's role as a democratic institution where art could be enjoyed by all.

Napoleon's Influence on the Collections:

- Napoleon Bonaparte played a crucial role in expanding the Louvre's collections during his military campaigns. Through conquests and diplomatic exchanges, he brought numerous works of art and artifacts to the museum, including such treasures as the Wedding at Cana, taken from Italy, and the Apollo Belvedere. His actions not only enriched the museum's holdings but also positioned the Louvre as a symbol of French power and cultural dominance.

Architectural Evolution with the Louvre Pyramid:

- One of the most visually striking and controversial additions to the Louvre was the glass Pyramid, designed by architect I. M. Pei and inaugurated in 1989.

This modernist structure, set within the historic courtyard, was initially met with skepticism but has since become an emblem of the Louvre. It symbolizes the museum's ongoing adaptation to contemporary needs while respecting its rich historical backdrop.

Expansion of Space and Collections:

- Over the years, the Louvre has continuously expanded its physical space and diversified its collections to accommodate an ever-increasing flow of visitors and to reflect a broader spectrum of global art. New wings and departments have been added, such as the Islamic Art wing in 2012, enhancing the museum's ability to showcase a wider array of cultures and histories. These expansions help the Louvre maintain its relevance and appeal as a global cultural institution.

The Louvre During War and Peace

The Louvre's history is a poignant reflection of its resilience and adaptation through both tumultuous and tranquil periods. This iconic museum has faced significant challenges during wars, yet it has continually emerged as a symbol of cultural strength and renewal.

Protecting Art During World War II:

- As World War II threatened Europe, the staff at the Louvre took extraordinary measures to protect the museum's invaluable collection. Anticipating the potential for looting or destruction, curators orchestrated a massive evacuation of artworks. Masterpieces like the Mona Lisa and the Venus de Milo were carefully packed and transported to various secure locations across France. This meticulous effort ensured that these treasures were kept safe from Nazi forces, showcasing the dedication and bravery of the museum's staff to safeguard humanity's heritage.

Post-War Recovery and Restoration:

- After the war, the Louvre played a crucial role in France's cultural and emotional recovery. The museum not only repaired physical damages to its structure but also focused on restoring the artworks that had suffered during the war. Reopening the Louvre and returning the artworks to their rightful place became a powerful symbol of resilience and renewal, reaffirming the museum's role in the heart of French culture.

Advancements in Peaceful Times:

- In times of peace, the Louvre has not remained static but has instead pursued ambitious expansions and modernizations. These include architectural developments like the addition of the Louvre Pyramid, as well as policy changes aimed at enhancing the visitor experience. The museum has also focused on diversifying its exhibitions and expanding its global reach, ensuring that it remains relevant and accessible to an international audience.

Symbolic Significance Through the Ages:

- Throughout its history, the Louvre has stood as more than just a museum. It is a testament to the enduring power of art and culture through both war and peace. The museum's ability to preserve and celebrate art, even in the face of adversity, offers a powerful narrative about the importance of cultural heritage. It reminds us that art is not merely for aesthetic appreciation but serves as a beacon of hope and a repository of human achievement across generations.

CHAPTER 3: MASTERPIECES OF THE LOUVRE

Must-See Treasures: Mona Lisa and Beyond

The Louvre houses some of the world's most celebrated masterpieces, drawing millions of visitors each year. While the Mona Lisa is often at the center of this artistic pilgrimage, the museum's vast collection offers many other treasures worth exploring.

Leonardo da Vinci's Mona Lisa:

- The Mona Lisa's allure is not just about her enigmatic smile. Leonardo da Vinci's masterpiece is renowned for its revolutionary use of technique, including sfumato, which creates a soft, gradual transition of colors, allowing for a more realistic portrayal of the human face. The painting's fame is amplified by its rich history of theft and recovery, adding a layer of intrigue that continues to captivate the public. Understanding these aspects helps appreciate why the Mona Lisa remains one of the most admired works in the world.

Other Iconic Works:

- The Louvre is also home to other monumental works that each carry their own historical and artistic significance:

    o **Venus de Milo:** This ancient Greek statue is celebrated for its classical beauty and mysterious origin, lacking arms yet still conveying a strong sense of motion and grace.

    o **Winged Victory of Samothrace:** Standing majestically atop a ship's prow, this sculpture symbolizes triumph and is acclaimed for its dynamic composition and realistic portrayal of drapery.

    o **The Coronation of Napoleon:** Jacques-Louis David's massive painting captures the grandeur and ceremony of Napoleon Bonaparte's coronation, offering insight into French history and the artist's meticulous attention to detail.

Viewing Tips:

- To fully enjoy these pieces, consider visiting during off-peak hours, such as early mornings or late evenings on Wednesdays and Fridays when the museum is open late. Positioning yourself strategically can also enhance your viewing experience; for example, standing a few steps back from the Mona Lisa allows a broader view, avoiding the reflection from its protective glass.

Beyond the Highlights:

- While the Mona Lisa and other famous pieces draw significant attention, the Louvre's collection is vast and varied, featuring works from nearly every civilization on earth. Visitors are encouraged to venture beyond the well-trodden paths to discover lesser-known but equally fascinating items, such as the Code of Hammurabi or the Egyptian antiquities. These pieces offer a deeper understanding of the breadth and diversity of human history and artistic expression housed within the museum.

Hidden Gems: Lesser-Known Wonders

While the Louvre is home to some of the world's most iconic artworks, it also offers an array of lesser-known treasures that provide a unique and personal exploration experience. Delving into these overlooked masterpieces can enrich your visit, offering new perspectives and a quieter journey through the museum.

Overlooked Masterpieces:

- **Liberty Leading the People by Delacroix**: This powerful painting, often overshadowed by more famous neighbors, captures the spirit of the French Revolution with dramatic intensity and emotion. Its dynamic composition and historical significance make it a must-see for those interested in French history and romantic art.

- **The Lacemaker by Vermeer**: Small in size but rich in detail, Vermeer's depiction of a young woman absorbed in her craft is a study in focus and delicacy. This painting is a perfect example of Vermeer's mastery of light and texture, offering a serene contrast to the grander narratives found elsewhere in the museum.

Lesser-Known Galleries:

- The Islamic Art section is one of the Louvre's most visually stunning yet underexplored areas. Housing thousands of objects that span over a thousand years and across three continents, this gallery showcases intricate ceramics, textiles, and metalworks that reflect the rich cultural heritage of the Islamic world. The space itself, covered by an undulating golden roof, is a work of art that complements the treasures it holds.

Rotating and Temporary Exhibits:

- The Louvre regularly hosts temporary exhibitions that bring rare or traveling works to the public. These exhibits are a chance to see something truly unique and temporary, adding an element of discovery and surprise to your visit. Checking the museum's schedule ahead of time can help you catch these limited-time displays.

Quiet Spaces and Hidden Gems:

- For those seeking a more contemplative experience, the Louvre offers several quieter corners where lesser-known works are displayed. These areas provide a respite from the bustling crowds and allow for more intimate interactions with the art. One such place is the lower ground floor of the Sully wing, where smaller, delicate artifacts and medieval remnants are thoughtfully presented away from the main thoroughfares.

Thematic Exploration of the Louvre: A Journey Through Time

Navigating the Louvre by historical period provides a structured, meaningful way to experience the museum's vast collection. By following the evolution of human creativity, visitors can gain deeper insights into the interconnectedness of art across different ages.

Begin with Ancient Civilizations:

- Start your journey in the **Egyptian Antiquities** section, home to artifacts that represent the beginnings of human expression.

From the grandeur of the Great Sphinx of Tanis to intricately carved sarcophagi, this area lays the foundation for understanding how early civilizations viewed life, death, and the afterlife. Following this, explore the **Mesopotamian Art** gallery, which showcases early writing systems, sculptures, and architecture from the cradle of civilization. These ancient works offer a window into the roots of human culture and creativity, setting the stage for everything that follows.

Transition to the Renaissance:

- Next, move to the **Renaissance galleries**, where the focus shifts to the artistic rebirth in Europe. Works by **Leonardo da Vinci**, **Michelangelo**, and **Raphael** reflect the cultural awakening that bridged the Middle Ages and the modern era.

These masterpieces, such as da Vinci's *Virgin and Child with Saint Anne* and Michelangelo's *Dying Slave*, showcase the human form in ways that had never been seen before, emphasizing realism, balance, and beauty. This section is crucial for understanding the link between the classical world and the modern age.

Explore the Baroque and Romantic Periods:

- Continue to the emotionally charged works of the **Baroque** and **Romantic** periods. Here, artists like **Peter Paul Rubens**, **Théodore Géricault**, and **Eugène Delacroix** pushed the boundaries of art, exploring drama, movement, and intense emotion. Rubens' *The Consequences of War* and Delacroix's *The Death of Sardanapalus* are prime examples of how art from these periods conveyed complex narratives and stirred powerful emotions. These works offer a sharp contrast to the more harmonious Renaissance pieces, reflecting the tumultuous times in which they were created.

Thematic Exploration:

- For a more focused experience, consider a **thematic tour** of the Louvre. Themes like **power**, **religion**, or **nature** can be traced across different time periods and artistic styles. For example, you can explore how depictions of rulers evolved from the imposing **Pharaohs of Ancient Egypt** to the glorified portraits of **Napoleon** in works like *The Coronation of Napoleon* by Jacques-Louis David. This approach offers a deeper, more reflective understanding of recurring themes in art, encouraging visitors to see connections between pieces that span centuries.

CHAPTER 4: THEMATIC TOURS INSIDE THE LOUVRE

The Romantic's Path: Love and Mystery in Art

The Louvre is not just a museum of history and grandeur—it also offers a deep exploration of human emotions, particularly love, passion, and mystery. This curated tour leads you through artworks that evoke these powerful themes, inviting a more personal and emotional connection to the pieces on display.

Psyche Revived by Cupid's Kiss by Antonio Canova:

- Begin with **Psyche Revived by Cupid's Kiss**, a marble sculpture by **Antonio Canova** that perfectly captures the moment of love and devotion. The delicate curves of Psyche and Cupid entwined in an eternal embrace showcase the beauty of romance. Canova's exquisite craftsmanship brings to life a scene filled with tenderness and longing, reminding visitors of the timeless nature of love as both fragile and powerful.

The Wedding Feast at Cana by Veronese:

- Next, stand before the grand canvas of **The Wedding Feast at Cana** by **Paolo Veronese**. This vibrant and lively scene, though often overlooked due to the nearby presence of the Mona Lisa, tells the story of a marriage celebration filled with love and mystery. The scale and intricate details of the painting, from the expressions of the guests to the subtle divine intervention, reveal the layers of joy, celebration, and deeper symbolism, blending human and spiritual love in one extravagant banquet.

Gabrielle d'Estrées and One of Her Sisters:

- Continue with the enigmatic painting **Gabrielle d'Estrées and One of Her Sisters**, a work filled with secrets and symbolism. This intriguing portrait captures the two women in a provocative pose, and its hidden meanings—tied to love, fidelity, and even political intrigue—draw viewers into a world of mystery.

The intimate gestures and expressions raise questions about the relationship between the subjects, inviting visitors to look deeper into the layers of love and secrecy woven into the painting.

The Coronation of Napoleon by Jacques-Louis David:

- Conclude your tour with **The Coronation of Napoleon** by **Jacques-Louis David**, a monumental painting that explores the complex interplay of love, power, and loyalty. Though primarily a political statement, the artwork also portrays Napoleon's relationship with his wife Josephine, who is depicted with grace and dignity. This moment of grandeur, where love intertwines with ambition and authority, ties together the tour's themes of romance and the mysteries of human relationships in a dramatic, historical context.

The Connoisseur's Route: Masterpieces and their Masters

For those who truly appreciate the brilliance behind each brushstroke, the Louvre offers a wealth of masterpieces created by the greatest artists in history. This curated tour dives deep into the technical mastery, emotional depth, and historical significance of these celebrated works, allowing art enthusiasts and history buffs to connect with the genius behind them.

The Mona Lisa by Leonardo da Vinci:

- Begin your journey with **The Mona Lisa**, arguably the most famous painting in the world. But beyond its fame lies Leonardo da Vinci's unparalleled technical mastery. His innovative use of **sfumato**, a technique that allows for soft transitions between colors, creates the illusion of depth and realism in the figure's face. The Mona Lisa's enduring mystique is further enhanced by her ambiguous expression and the complex layers of light and shadow that make her come to life.

Da Vinci's work revolutionized portrait painting, and understanding these innovations allows visitors to see why this small, seemingly simple portrait continues to captivate the world.

The Raft of the Medusa by Théodore Géricault:

- Next, confront the raw emotion and dramatic realism of **The Raft of the Medusa** by **Théodore Géricault**. This massive canvas, based on a real-life shipwreck, is a powerful example of Romantic art at its finest. Géricault spent months researching the event, even visiting morgues to study dead bodies, in order to accurately depict the suffering and desperation of the survivors. The painting's dynamic composition and masterful use of light and shadow create an intense, visceral scene that leaves a lasting impact. It also serves as a sharp critique of political incompetence, making it both a work of artistic genius and a piece of social commentary.

Liberty Leading the People by Eugène Delacroix:

- From political critique to revolutionary fervor, continue with **Liberty Leading the People** by **Eugène Delacroix**. This iconic painting captures the spirit of the July Revolution of 1830, where Liberty, personified as a fearless woman, leads the charge over a barricade. Delacroix's bold use of color and movement injects a sense of urgency and passion into the scene. Every detail, from the fluttering flag to the lifeless bodies on the ground, serves to emphasize the chaos and sacrifice of revolution. Delacroix's dynamic composition and vivid storytelling make this piece a defining work of the Romantic movement.

The Lacemaker by Johannes Vermeer:

- Conclude your tour on a quieter, more intimate note with **The Lacemaker** by **Johannes Vermeer**. Vermeer's meticulous attention to detail is evident in this small yet captivating painting.

His delicate use of light, so characteristic of his work, bathes the scene in a soft glow, enhancing the serenity and concentration of the young woman as she works on her lace. Vermeer's precise brushwork and his ability to capture the beauty of everyday life elevate this seemingly simple scene into a timeless masterpiece. The painting's quietness contrasts sharply with the previous works, offering a moment of reflection and appreciation for the intricacies of life.

Family Friendly: Engaging the Young Art Lover

Exploring the Louvre with children can be both fun and educational when focused on interactive, visually stimulating works that ignite curiosity. This family-friendly route highlights areas of the museum that will captivate young minds, making art accessible and exciting.

Egyptian Antiquities:

- Start your adventure in the **Egyptian Antiquities** section, where children can discover the mysteries of ancient Egypt.

The display of mummies, statues of gods, and hieroglyphic carvings are sure to spark their imagination. This section offers an engaging way to introduce kids to history, encouraging them to learn about the fascinating world of pharaohs, tombs, and ancient rituals.

Galerie d'Apollon:

- Next, head to the **Galerie d'Apollon**, a stunning gallery filled with golden ceilings and grand artwork. Children will be amazed by the sparkling décor and stories of French royalty. The opulent surroundings, with their tales of kings and queens, will transport young visitors to a world of castles and crowns, making history come alive in a visually captivating way.

The Winged Victory of Samothrace:

- Continue with the **Winged Victory of Samothrace**, a dramatic sculpture that stands at the top of a grand staircase.

This ancient Greek masterpiece, with its flowing form and sense of motion, is not only visually striking but also provides a chance to introduce children to the mythology behind the art. Kids can imagine the powerful winged figure soaring above them, adding a sense of excitement and adventure to their visit.

Interactive Digital Displays:

- Finally, finish the tour by visiting galleries with **interactive digital displays**. These hands-on tools allow children to engage with the artwork in a modern, fun way. They can explore art through touch screens, learn stories behind the pieces, and even play games related to the exhibits. This interactive approach ensures a memorable experience, making the art more relatable and enjoyable for young visitors.

Chapter 5: Architectural Wonders

Palatial Splendors: The Louvre as a Royal Residence

Before it became the world's most famous museum, the Louvre was a royal palace, rich in history and architectural evolution. This journey through its transformation reveals the grandeur and significance of its role as a symbol of royal power and culture.

The Medieval Fortress of King Philip II:

- The Louvre's origins trace back to the 12th century when **King Philip II** built it as a fortress to defend Paris. Some remnants of this medieval stronghold, such as the original **moat and stone foundations**, are still visible in the museum today. These preserved elements offer a glimpse into the Louvre's military past, showcasing its initial purpose as a fortification rather than a cultural landmark. Exploring these areas helps readers appreciate the monumental shift from fortress to palace.

Royal Expansions under Francis I and Louis XIV:

- The architectural transformation began under **King Francis I**, who sought to modernize the Louvre, initiating its evolution from a medieval stronghold into a symbol of royal prestige. Under his reign, the Renaissance-inspired expansions introduced classical elements and housed France's burgeoning art collection. **Louis XIV** further elevated the Louvre's status, transforming it into a royal residence with grand halls and ornate rooms designed to display the monarchy's wealth and cultural dominance. These expansions signaled the monarchy's desire to solidify its power through both architecture and art, creating a palace that reflected France's growing influence.

Napoleon III's Apartments:

- One of the most opulent parts of the Louvre that still exists today is the **Napoleon III Apartments**, a dazzling representation of 19th-century luxury.

These rooms, preserved in their original splendor, are adorned with gold accents, crystal chandeliers, and richly decorated furnishings. Walking through these spaces transports visitors to a time of imperial grandeur, offering a vivid glimpse into the lavish lifestyle of French royalty at its peak.

Exterior Facades and Architectural Styles:

- The Louvre's **exterior facades** are masterpieces in themselves, blending **Renaissance** and **Baroque** architectural styles that reflect the artistic tastes of different monarchs. The intricate carvings, grand arches, and monumental scale of the Louvre's exterior were designed to impress and symbolize the power and refinement of the French monarchy. By examining these facades, readers can appreciate not just the art inside the museum, but the Louvre itself as an important historical artifact and an enduring symbol of France's royal and cultural legacy.

Modern Additions: The Pyramid and Contemporary Flares

The Louvre's classical architecture, steeped in centuries of history, took a bold step into the future with the introduction of modern elements that redefined the museum's presence and visitor experience. These additions reflect the museum's adaptability and willingness to evolve, while still honoring its past.

The Controversial Pyramid by I. M. Pei:

- One of the most striking additions to the Louvre is the **glass pyramid**, designed by **I. M. Pei** and unveiled in 1989. Its introduction was met with controversy, as many critics felt that the modern glass structure clashed with the classical aesthetic of the Louvre's historic facades. However, the pyramid has since become a symbol of the museum's evolution. Its transparent design not only redefined the museum's entrance but also represents openness and accessibility, inviting the public to experience the Louvre in a new light.

This contrast between the old and the new has sparked debates about the coexistence of modern and historical architecture, yet the pyramid stands as a powerful statement of the museum's adaptability.

A Bridge Between Past and Future:

- The pyramid's clean, minimalist lines stand in stark contrast to the ornate, historical surroundings of the Louvre, but it does more than create visual tension. It serves as a metaphor for the Louvre's mission to honor its rich heritage while embracing the future. The pyramid's geometric design, based on ancient Egyptian principles, also subtly connects it to the history of civilization, bridging eras and reminding visitors that the museum is a living, breathing institution that must continue to grow and adapt.

Carrousel du Louvre:

- Another modern addition is the **Carrousel du Louvre**, an underground shopping mall that seamlessly blends art, commerce, and modern design.

With its sleek architecture and contemporary art installations, this space offers a more commercial yet artistic element to the Louvre experience. It also houses the **Inverted Pyramid**, an upside-down glass structure that has become a modern architectural icon in its own right. These additions demonstrate how the museum integrates practical, modern spaces with its cultural mission, enriching the visitor experience.

The Inverted Pyramid:

- The **Inverted Pyramid**, located beneath the ground floor, provides a visually stunning contrast to the classical art above it. Its unique form captures light in dynamic ways, creating an almost futuristic atmosphere within the Louvre's historic setting. This addition, while subtle, is emblematic of the museum's ongoing commitment to innovation, offering visitors a fresh, modern perspective even as they stand surrounded by centuries-old masterpieces.

Sculptures and Gardens: Art Beyond the Walls

While the Louvre's galleries are filled with some of the most celebrated works of art, the museum's beauty extends beyond its indoor spaces. The sculptures and gardens surrounding the Louvre offer visitors a chance to experience art in natural, open-air settings, providing a peaceful yet inspiring environment.

The Cour Marly and Cour Puget:

- Begin your outdoor art journey in the **Cour Marly** and **Cour Puget**, two stunning open-air galleries that are part of the Louvre's indoor-outdoor experience. These spaces feature magnificent French sculptures bathed in natural light, with large glass ceilings enhancing the grandeur of the statues. The blend of classical architecture and dynamic sculpture in these airy courtyards creates a unique atmosphere where visitors can admire works like **Marly Horses** and **Milo of Croton**, all while enjoying the sense of openness.

The Jardin des Tuileries:

- Just steps from the Louvre lies the **Jardin des Tuileries**, a historic garden designed by **André Le Nôtre** in the 17th century. As visitors stroll through these beautiful grounds, they'll encounter sculptures by modern artists such as **Rodin** and **Maillol**, creating a harmonious dialogue between past and present. The gardens are more than just a picturesque retreat—they are an extension of the Louvre's collection, offering a tranquil yet immersive experience that combines nature with artistic expression. Visitors can unwind on one of the many benches while admiring the art and the carefully manicured landscapes that reflect centuries of French gardening tradition.

Arc de Triomphe du Carrousel:

- In the Louvre's courtyard stands the **Arc de Triomphe du Carrousel**, a triumphal arch that serves as a symbol of French military victories.

Built to commemorate Napoleon's successes, this masterpiece is adorned with intricate sculptures and bas-reliefs that depict key historical events. The arch not only adds architectural beauty to the Louvre's exterior but also connects visitors to France's storied past, standing as a reminder of the museum's deep ties to the nation's history.

Exterior Statues and Fountains:

- Throughout the Louvre's exterior, visitors will find **statues and fountains** that enhance the visual composition of the museum's grand facades. These works of art, set against the backdrop of the Louvre's magnificent architecture, provide a seamless blend of art and environment. From the majestic fountains in the Tuileries to the sculptures that line the museum's courtyards, these outdoor pieces invite visitors to engage with the art in new ways, offering a full sensory experience that extends beyond the museum's walls.

CHAPTER 6: CULTURAL IMMERSION

Art Workshops and Lectures: Learn from Experts

For those looking to deepen their connection to art, the Louvre offers a variety of workshops and lectures that go beyond simple observation, giving visitors the opportunity to engage with art in more meaningful and interactive ways. These programs are designed to enrich the museum experience by blending education, creativity, and hands-on learning.

Art Workshops:

- The Louvre provides a wide range of **art workshops**, where visitors can learn techniques such as **sketching**, **painting**, and **sculpture**. Under the guidance of skilled instructors, participants can practice drawing from life, inspired by the museum's rich collections, or try their hand at modeling sculptures based on classical forms. These workshops offer a hands-on opportunity to not only observe great works of art but to immerse yourself in the creative process, making your visit more interactive and fulfilling.

73

Specialized Lectures on Art History:

- For those who are more academically inclined, the Louvre offers **specialized lectures** on topics such as **Renaissance art**, **ancient civilizations**, and **modern artistic movements**. Presented by scholars, curators, and art historians, these lectures provide deep insights into the historical and cultural contexts of the artworks, offering a more nuanced understanding of the museum's vast collection. Whether you are interested in learning more about a specific period or want to explore art's influence on society, these lectures offer an intellectual journey through the world of art.

Thematic Art Tours and Guided Workshops:

- One of the most enriching ways to experience the Louvre is through a **thematic art tour** followed by a guided workshop. Participants can explore a specific theme, such as portraiture or mythological art, with a curator or expert guide, and then apply what they've learned in a practical art session.

Surrounded by the very works that inspired their creations, visitors gain a deeper appreciation for the artistic techniques and concepts discussed during the tour.

Accessible for All Skill Levels:

- These workshops and lectures are designed to be accessible to everyone, from beginners to seasoned art enthusiasts. Whether you're picking up a brush for the first time or you've been studying art for years, the Louvre's programs cater to a wide range of skill levels. This ensures that anyone with an interest in art can participate and walk away with a richer understanding of the creative and historical forces behind the masterpieces they've seen.

Photographic Opportunities: Capturing Timeless Moments

The Louvre offers countless photographic opportunities, both inside its majestic halls and throughout its beautifully designed outdoor spaces. With a bit of guidance, visitors can capture stunning images that reflect the museum's grandeur and the essence of their visit.

Best Locations for Photography:

- **The Glass Pyramid**: Start by capturing the **Louvre Pyramid**, a modern architectural icon framed by the historic facades of the museum. The contrast between the sleek glass and the classical architecture creates a visually striking image, especially during sunrise or sunset when the light adds a golden hue.

- **Grand Galleries**: Inside the Louvre, head to the **Denon Wing**, home to the **Mona Lisa** and other masterpieces. The gallery's high ceilings and ornate decor provide a beautiful backdrop for any photograph.

- **Courtyards**: Don't miss the **Cour Puget** and **Cour Marly**, where open-air galleries bathe stunning sculptures in natural light, offering perfect conditions for well-lit, detailed shots.

Tips for Photographing Masterpieces:

- To photograph iconic pieces like the **Mona Lisa** or **Venus de Milo**, aim to visit early in the morning or later in the day to avoid heavy crowds.

Position yourself at a slight angle to avoid reflections from protective glass, and use zoom features to focus on details while maintaining a respectful distance. Be mindful of other visitors, ensuring your photography doesn't obstruct their view or disrupt their experience.

Outdoor Photography Opportunities:

- The **Jardin des Tuileries**, adjacent to the Louvre, is an ideal spot for outdoor photography. Here, you can capture a blend of nature, sculptures, and fountains with the museum's facade in the background. The symmetrical paths and carefully manicured gardens offer endless opportunities for beautiful compositions.

- In the **courtyards** of the Louvre, you'll find impressive statues, fountains, and the **Arc de Triomphe du Carrousel**, all of which provide excellent subjects for photography. The architecture itself, with its grand arches and intricate stonework, can make for stunning wide-angle shots.

Practical Photography Tips:

- **Lighting**: Take advantage of natural light in the Louvre's courtyards or the glass-covered **Cour Marly**. Indoors, use indirect light from large windows to avoid harsh shadows or overexposure.

- **Angles and Framing**: Experiment with angles to find the most flattering perspective. For large sculptures or grand spaces, try shooting from a low angle to emphasize their scale. When photographing art, use framing techniques to isolate the subject and reduce distractions.

- **Equipment**: Whether you're using a smartphone or a DSLR, adjust your camera's settings to match the conditions. In lower light, increase your ISO or use a tripod for steady shots. For smartphones, enable grid lines to help with alignment and composition.

Night at the Museum: Evening Events and Special Tours

Visiting the Louvre during evening hours presents a unique and intimate opportunity to explore its world-class collections. Whether you're seeking a peaceful gallery stroll or a curated cultural event, the museum at night offers a completely different experience that enhances the magic of this iconic space.

Wednesday and Friday Evening Visits:

- On **Wednesdays and Fridays**, the Louvre extends its hours until 9:45 PM, transforming the museum into a quieter, more serene space. As the crowds thin, visitors can take their time wandering through the galleries, absorbing the art without the usual hustle and bustle. The soft lighting and tranquil atmosphere make for a relaxed and deeply personal connection with the artworks, creating an unforgettable evening experience.

Nocturnes: Special Nighttime Events:

- The Louvre also hosts special evening events known as **Nocturnes**, where live performances, art discussions, and guided tours combine to offer a dynamic cultural experience. These events turn the museum into a lively, artistic hub, with activities that might range from classical music concerts to contemporary dance performances, all staged against the backdrop of the museum's masterpieces. **Nocturnes** bring art and entertainment together in a way that transforms a traditional museum visit into something truly extraordinary.

Exclusive Night Tours:

- For a more intimate and immersive experience, consider joining one of the **exclusive night tours**. These thematic tours, conducted under the museum's subtle evening lighting, reveal the artworks in a different way, highlighting textures, shadows, and details that may not be as apparent during the day.

- These tours often focus on specific themes or periods, allowing visitors to explore the art from a fresh perspective, enhancing the emotional and visual impact.

Limited-Time Evening Exhibitions and Pop-Up Events:

- The Louvre also occasionally hosts **limited-time evening exhibitions** or pop-up events, offering visitors a chance to engage with the museum in exclusive ways. These events might feature newly curated exhibits, interactive art installations, or guest lectures, providing a deeper, more enriching cultural experience. Participating in these rare opportunities adds an extra layer of excitement to a night at the Louvre, making it a visit to remember.

CHAPTER 7: DINING AND SHOPPING

Culinary Arts: Best Eateries Within and Near the Louvre

A visit to the Louvre is not only a feast for the eyes but can also be a delightful culinary experience. Here's a guide to some of the best dining options within the museum and nearby, perfect for enhancing your artistic journey with Parisian flavors.

On-Site Cafés and Restaurants:

- **Café Marly**: Located in the museum's Richelieu Wing, **Café Marly** offers refined French cuisine paired with stunning views of the **Louvre Pyramid** and courtyards. With its elegant interior and outdoor terrace, it's a perfect spot to relax and enjoy a leisurely meal after exploring the museum. The menu features classic dishes like foie gras and duck confit, all while soaking in the grandeur of the Louvre's architecture.

- **Le Café Richelieu**: Situated on the museum's upper floor, **Le Café Richelieu** provides another excellent option, offering French specialties with a view over the Cour Napoleon. Visitors can enjoy a blend of traditional and contemporary dishes, making it a convenient yet stylish dining choice without leaving the museum.

Nearby Bistros and Brasseries:

- **Le Fumoir**: Just a short walk from the Louvre,

Le Fumoir offers a quintessential Parisian dining experience, blending cozy charm with a vibrant atmosphere. Known for its classic French dishes like beef tartare and fresh seafood, it's the perfect place to unwind with a glass of wine after a day of art exploration. The intimate setting and proximity to the museum make it a favorite among both locals and visitors.

- **La Régalade**: Another great option nearby is **La Régalade**, a modern bistro serving hearty French fare. Its relaxed yet refined ambiance makes it ideal for those wanting an authentic taste of Paris without the formality. Dishes are crafted from fresh, seasonal ingredients, with an emphasis on generous portions and rich flavors.

Quick Bites Near the Louvre:

- For visitors who prefer something quick and casual, there are several great options within walking distance. Grab a sandwich or pastry from **Paul** or **Maison Pradier**, both located near the **Tuileries Gardens**, where you can enjoy a picnic in the park while admiring the city's scenery. Food trucks around the area often offer crepes, sandwiches, or croissants—perfect for a quick, affordable bite on the go.

Pastries and Desserts:

- No visit to Paris is complete without indulging in some sweet treats. Head to nearby pâtisseries like **Angelina**, famous for its decadent hot chocolate and **Mont Blanc** dessert, or **Pierre Hermé**, known for exquisite macarons and other French pastries.

These indulgences offer a delicious way to complement the artistry of your museum visit, making the experience even more memorable.

A visit to the Louvre offers more than just artistic inspiration—it also provides opportunities to take home beautiful, sophisticated souvenirs that capture the essence of your experience. From art prints to luxury items, here's how you can commemorate your visit with meaningful keepsakes.

Louvre's Official Gift Shops:

- The Louvre's **official gift shops** are the perfect place to find exclusive items that directly reflect the museum's renowned collection. You can purchase high-quality **art prints** of famous works such as the **Mona Lisa** or **Winged Victory**, allowing you to bring home a piece of art history. In addition to prints, the shops offer beautifully bound **books**, **postcards**, and **replicas** of sculptures and other iconic works, all museum-endorsed to ensure authenticity and quality.

These items make for timeless mementos that encapsulate the beauty of the Louvre.

Carrousel du Louvre Artisan Shops:

- For something more unique, the **Carrousel du Louvre** mall is home to artisan shops that feature handcrafted items inspired by Parisian art and culture. Here, you can find **handcrafted jewelry**, **decorative textiles**, and **home décor** items that reflect the artistry of the museum and its surroundings. These shops offer a level of sophistication beyond typical tourist fare, allowing you to take home a truly distinctive piece that captures the elegance and creativity of Paris.

Bookstores and Scholarly Publications:

- For visitors with a passion for art history, nearby **bookstores** provide a treasure trove of rare **art books**, **catalogs**, and **scholarly publications**. These carefully curated selections offer a deeper dive into the world of art, allowing you to extend your learning long after your visit.

Whether you're interested in Renaissance masterpieces or modern artistic movements, these bookstores give you the opportunity to explore art in greater detail through literature.

Local Boutiques for Luxury Goods:

- Expand your shopping experience by visiting local Parisian **boutiques** that specialize in luxury items such as **French fashion**, **perfumes**, or **high-end stationery**. These refined products embody the elegance of French craftsmanship, offering a sophisticated touch to your souvenir collection. Whether you're indulging in a chic Parisian handbag, a signature French fragrance, or beautifully designed stationery, these luxury items serve as lasting reminders of your visit to one of the most cultured cities in the world.

CHAPTER 8: TIPS AND TRICKS FOR THE SAVVY TRAVELER

Avoiding the Crowds: Insider Secrets

Visiting the Louvre can be an overwhelming experience due to the sheer number of visitors it attracts, but with the right strategies, you can enjoy a more peaceful and personal journey through its galleries. Here are some insider tips to help you avoid the crowds and make the most of your visit.

1. Visit During Off-Peak Hours:

- One of the best ways to avoid crowds is to plan your visit during **off-peak hours**. Arriving early in the morning right when the museum opens, or late in the afternoon, especially on **Wednesdays** and **Fridays** when the Louvre stays open until 9:45 PM, will give you a much quieter experience. These times tend to have fewer visitors, allowing you to explore the galleries with more ease and tranquility.

2. Purchase Tickets Online in Advance:

- Avoid long entry lines by **purchasing tickets online** ahead of time. This simple step can save you significant wait time, particularly during peak tourist seasons. Booking in advance also gives you the flexibility to plan your day and ensures a smoother, more efficient start to your museum visit.

3. Explore Lesser-Known Wings:

- While most visitors flock to see the Mona Lisa or the Venus de Milo, there are many other hidden gems throughout the museum. Explore the **Islamic Art** wing, the **Decorative Arts** section, or the **Sully Wing**, which tend to attract fewer crowds. These areas house exquisite collections and often provide a quieter, more intimate atmosphere for art appreciation.

4. Visit During the Off-Season:

- The Louvre is significantly less crowded during **off-season months** (November to February), making it an ideal time for a relaxed visit.

Winter in Paris sees fewer tourists overall, and the museum offers a more serene environment to explore without the usual bustling crowds. Plus, the cooler weather is perfect for spending time indoors, soaking in centuries of art and history.

The Art of Appreciation: Enhancing Your Viewing Experience

A visit to the Louvre can be overwhelming due to its vast collection, but with the right techniques, you can cultivate a deeper connection with the artwork and make your experience more enriching. Here are some ways to enhance your appreciation of the art you encounter.

1. Focus on a Select Number of Works:

- Rather than trying to see everything, focus on a few select masterpieces. This approach promotes **quality over quantity**, allowing you to take your time and engage more deeply with each piece. By concentrating on fewer works, you can develop a richer, more personal connection with the art, appreciating the details and emotions behind the masterpieces.

2. Research Before You Visit:

- Enhance your experience by **researching the history and symbolism** behind key works before you visit. Arriving with context and insight into the pieces you'll see, such as the artist's background or the significance of the imagery, allows you to engage more thoughtfully. This preparation makes the viewing experience more rewarding, as you'll understand not just what you're seeing, but why it matters.

3. Use Audio Guides or Museum Apps:

- The Louvre offers **audio guides and mobile apps** that provide expert commentary and in-depth information about the artworks. These resources offer valuable insights into the significance, context, and techniques behind specific works, helping you appreciate the nuances that might otherwise go unnoticed. Using these tools can transform your visit into an educational experience, deepening your understanding of the art.

4. Take Time for Reflection:

- One of the most powerful ways to appreciate art is to **sit quietly in front of a favorite piece** and allow time for reflection. Taking a few moments to absorb the work's emotional and aesthetic impact without feeling rushed encourages a mindful approach to art appreciation. This pause for personal interpretation allows you to connect with the artwork on a deeper, more emotional level.

Accessibility and Assistance: Ensuring a Smooth Visit

The Louvre is committed to providing an inclusive experience for all visitors, offering a range of services and facilities to ensure that everyone, including those with disabilities or special needs, can enjoy the museum comfortably. Here are some key tips and features that make the Louvre accessible and convenient for all.

1. Accessibility Features:

- The Louvre offers extensive **accessibility features** such as **wheelchair ramps, elevators,** and

accessible entrances to make the museum navigable for visitors with mobility challenges.

These features ensure that every part of the museum is easily reachable, from its grand galleries to its more intimate exhibition spaces, allowing all visitors to explore the art without difficulty.

2. Free Services for Assistance:

- The museum provides several free services to enhance accessibility, including **wheelchair rentals** and **accessible parking** near the entrance. Visitors can take advantage of these offerings to ensure a smoother visit. There are also tactile tours available for those with visual impairments, allowing a more interactive experience. These services are designed to make the Louvre more welcoming and convenient for those requiring extra support.

3. Guided Tours and Staff Assistance:

- Visitors can book **guided tours** tailored to those with special needs or request assistance from museum staff, who are trained to provide support.

These services ensure that all parts of the museum, including less accessible areas, are available for exploration.

Whether it's help navigating a specific exhibit or providing additional context for an artwork, the staff is ready to assist to ensure an enjoyable visit.

4. Tips for Visiting with Children or Elderly Companions:

- For those visiting the Louvre with children or elderly companions, the museum offers **seating areas** throughout the galleries for rest. The **Cour Marly** and **Cour Puget** offer open spaces where visitors can take breaks and enjoy the art at a more relaxed pace. If frequent breaks are needed, planning routes with nearby seating areas can make the experience more comfortable for everyone involved.

CHAPTER 9: BEYOND THE LOUVRE

Parisian Art Scene: Other Must-Visit Locations

While the Louvre is a cornerstone of Parisian art, the city offers a wealth of other art destinations that deepen one's appreciation of its rich artistic heritage. Here are some must-visit locations for a broader, more immersive cultural experience.

1. Musée d'Orsay:

- A visit to the **Musée d'Orsay** is essential for anyone interested in the evolution of modern art. Housed in a beautifully converted **former railway station**, this museum boasts an exceptional collection of **Impressionist and Post-Impressionist masterpieces**. Works by **Monet**, **Van Gogh**, **Renoir**, and **Degas** grace the walls, showcasing the transformation of art from traditional to modern. The museum's grand setting, with its expansive ceilings and sweeping views of the Seine, adds to the dramatic presentation of these groundbreaking works.

2. Centre Pompidou:

- For those drawn to contemporary and avant-garde art, the **Centre Pompidou** is a must-see. Its **strikingly modern architecture**, with its exposed pipes and industrial design, stands in bold contrast to the classicism of the Louvre. Inside, the museum houses one of the largest collections of **modern and contemporary art** in Europe, featuring works by **Picasso**, **Duchamp**, and **Kandinsky**. The Centre Pompidou also hosts innovative exhibitions, installations, and performances, making it a vibrant space for exploring the cutting edge of the art world.

3. Musée de l'Orangerie:

- Nestled in the Tuileries Gardens, the **Musée de l'Orangerie** offers a more intimate and serene art experience. The museum is best known for its breathtaking display of **Monet's Water Lilies**, presented in two large, oval rooms that create an immersive environment. Visitors can lose themselves in the subtle color palettes and reflections of Monet's peaceful, natural scenes.

The museum also features works by **Renoir**, **Matisse**, and **Modigliani**, providing a harmonious blend of Impressionist and Post-Impressionist art.

4. Montmartre and the Musée de Montmartre:

- For a taste of Paris's bohemian art scene, a stroll through the **Montmartre** district is a must. Once home to artists like **Picasso**, **Toulouse-Lautrec**, and **Van Gogh**, this vibrant neighborhood is steeped in artistic history. Visit the **Musée de Montmartre** to learn more about the district's rich cultural past, and explore the local galleries that still thrive today. The lively streets, cafés, and artist studios make Montmartre an unforgettable experience for those who want to immerse themselves in the heart of Paris's artistic spirit.

While Paris is a treasure trove of art and culture, there are many enriching destinations just outside the city that complement a Louvre visit. These day trips offer visitors a chance to explore France's rich heritage through its stunning art, architecture, and history.

1. Versailles:

- A visit to the **Palace of Versailles** is a must for anyone interested in French royal history and **Baroque art**. The opulence of the **Hall of Mirrors**, the grandeur of the royal apartments, and the meticulously designed gardens by **André Le Nôtre** all provide a breathtaking exploration of French aristocratic life. Versailles is the pinnacle of French architecture and art, making it a perfect extension of the Louvre experience. From lavish tapestries to intricate ceiling frescoes, visitors can immerse themselves in the height of French cultural achievement.

2. Château de Fontainebleau:

- For a less-crowded yet equally impressive alternative to Versailles, consider visiting the **Château de Fontainebleau**, one of France's largest and oldest royal residences. This UNESCO World Heritage site offers a rich tapestry of **Renaissance art**, **Napoleonic history**, and French architecture. Fontainebleau was home to generations of French kings and emperors, and its halls are adorned with exquisite frescoes, gilded rooms, and the famous **Gallery of Francis I**, a masterpiece of Renaissance design. The château's peaceful atmosphere and fewer tourists provide a more relaxed and intimate experience of French royal history.

3. Giverny:

- For an art-focused day trip, head to **Giverny**, the home of **Claude Monet**. Visitors can explore **Monet's house** and the beautiful gardens that inspired his famous **Water Lilies** series.

Walking through the vibrant garden, with its Japanese bridge and blooming flowers, feels like stepping into one of Monet's paintings. This visit offers a unique, immersive connection to the art you've seen at the Louvre, giving you a chance to experience the landscapes that shaped one of the greatest artists in history.

4. Auvers-sur-Oise:

- Art lovers and Van Gogh enthusiasts should not miss **Auvers-sur-Oise**, the village where **Vincent van Gogh** spent his final days. This quiet village, just outside Paris, allows visitors to explore the house where Van Gogh lived, the **Auberge Ravoux**, and the **Church of Auvers**, famously painted by the artist. A visit here offers a deeply personal look at Van Gogh's life and his artistic process, as you follow in his footsteps and see the places that inspired his final works. It's a reflective and moving journey for those who wish to connect more closely with his legacy.

The Express Tour: Louvre Highlights in 2 Hours

For visitors with limited time, this two-hour itinerary covers the **Louvre's** most iconic works, ensuring you experience the museum's must-see pieces efficiently while still soaking in the grandeur of its collection.

1. Start with The Mona Lisa (Denon Wing):

- Begin your express tour at the **Mona Lisa**, located in the **Denon Wing**. As the world's most famous painting, it's a priority for any visit. To avoid the crowds, head straight to this masterpiece, positioning yourself strategically for a clear view of **Leonardo da Vinci's** enigmatic portrait.

2. The Winged Victory of Samothrace (Daru Staircase):

- After seeing the Mona Lisa, make your way to the **Winged Victory of Samothrace**, positioned dramatically at the top of the **Daru staircase**.

This ancient Greek sculpture, with its flowing drapery and sense of motion, is one of the most visually striking pieces in the museum and will add a dynamic, awe-inspiring moment to your tour.

3. Venus de Milo (Sully Wing):

- Continue to the **Sully Wing** to admire the **Venus de Milo**, another of the Louvre's emblematic masterpieces. This iconic statue of **Aphrodite** is a timeless symbol of classical beauty and elegance, offering visitors a glimpse into the grandeur of ancient Greek art.

4. End with Liberty Leading the People (Denon Wing):

- Conclude your tour back in the **Denon Wing** with **Eugène Delacroix's Liberty Leading the People**. This powerful painting celebrates the spirit of revolution and the fight for freedom, embodying French national pride. Ending here provides a strong cultural and emotional connection to the museum's French art collection.

A Full-Day Immersion: Masterpieces and Hidden Treasures

For art lovers wanting to dive deep into the Louvre's vast collection, this full-day itinerary balances must-see masterpieces with quieter, lesser-known treasures, ensuring a fulfilling and immersive experience.

1. Start with the Masterpieces:

- Begin your day early with the **Mona Lisa, Venus de Milo**, and **Winged Victory of Samothrace**. These iconic works are best visited in the morning before the museum gets crowded, allowing you to appreciate their details without the usual interruptions. By covering these essentials first, you'll have ample time for deeper exploration throughout the day.

2. Explore Egyptian Antiquities:

- After experiencing the highlights, head to the **Egyptian Antiquities** section for a quieter and more educational journey through ancient history.

Marvel at treasures such as the **Great Sphinx of Tanis**, **mummies**, and intricate **hieroglyphic** carvings. This collection offers a fascinating dive into one of the world's oldest civilizations and provides a rich contrast to the more famous works of European art.

3. Lunch at Café Marly:

- Take a break for lunch at **Café Marly**, offering a stunning view of the **Louvre Pyramid**. This elegant spot allows you to relax and reflect on the morning's discoveries, while soaking in the beauty of your surroundings. The calm setting and refined cuisine provide a well-deserved rest in the midst of your art-filled day.

4. Afternoon in the Islamic and Decorative Arts Sections:

- In the afternoon, venture into the **Islamic Art** and **Decorative Arts** sections. These often-overlooked collections feature exquisite textiles, ceramics, and metalwork, highlighting the beauty of craftsmanship across different cultures and time periods.

The intricate details and artistry of these pieces offer a rewarding exploration of artistic traditions outside the Western canon.

5. End with Reflection in Cour Puget or Cour Marly:

- Conclude your day in the serene **Cour Puget** or **Cour Marly**. These open-air galleries, filled with light and monumental sculptures, provide a peaceful, contemplative space to unwind. The blend of natural light and sculpture creates a visually stunning environment, offering the perfect setting for quiet reflection on your full-day immersion in the Louvre's masterpieces and hidden treasures.

Family Fun: Engaging the Kids with a Half-Day Tour

Visiting the Louvre with children can be a fun and enriching experience if the right artworks and activities are chosen. This half-day itinerary is designed to keep young visitors entertained with interactive and visually captivating displays, ensuring an enjoyable and educational family visit.

1. Start with the Egyptian Antiquities Section:

- Begin your visit in the **Egyptian Antiquities** section, where kids can marvel at mummies, intricately decorated tombs, and ancient artifacts. Objects like the **Sphinx of Tanis** and **sarcophagi** bring history to life, offering children an exciting glimpse into the world of ancient Egypt. This section offers a perfect mix of wonder and education, capturing the imaginations of young visitors while teaching them about ancient civilizations.

2. Visit The Winged Victory of Samothrace:

- Next, head to the **Winged Victory of Samothrace**, a dramatic sculpture that towers above the Daru staircase. Use this stop to introduce children to ancient **mythology** and heroic tales, explaining the significance of the goddess Nike and her role in Greek history. The statue's dynamic pose and sense of movement provide a captivating visual experience for kids, making art and history feel larger-than-life.

3. Explore the Galerie d'Apollon:

- Afterward, visit the **Galerie d'Apollon**, where royal crowns and sparkling jewels are sure to capture the attention of children. The dazzling display of opulence, including **Louis XIV's crowns** and other regal treasures, offers a fun opportunity for kids to see up-close the grandeur of French royalty. The bright, glittering objects are engaging for young visitors and provide a visual break from paintings and sculptures.

4. End with the Interactive Digital Displays:

- Conclude your visit with the **Interactive Digital Displays**, which allow kids to explore the Louvre's collection in a hands-on, modern format. These digital stations provide an engaging and fun way for children to interact with the art, offering games, quizzes, and virtual tours that help keep their attention and make learning more dynamic.

This thematic tour takes visitors through the Louvre's collection, focusing on powerful depictions of love and mythology. By exploring different expressions of love—romantic, celebratory, and complex—this tour offers an emotionally rich and culturally immersive experience.

1. Psyche Revived by Cupid's Kiss by Antonio Canova:

- Begin with **Psyche Revived by Cupid's Kiss**, a breathtaking marble sculpture by **Antonio Canova**. This work perfectly captures the tender moment when Cupid revives Psyche with a kiss, embodying the themes of **love, passion**, and **mythological storytelling**. The delicate intertwining of their bodies and the expression of pure emotion sets the tone for the rest of the tour, establishing a focus on the intimate and mythological aspects of love.

2. The Wedding Feast at Cana by Veronese:

- Next, visit **The Wedding Feast at Cana** by **Paolo Veronese**, a grand painting that showcases a **celebration of love** in a lively and vibrant scene.

Depicting the biblical story of Christ's first miracle at a wedding, this work highlights the joy and festivity that accompany love. The painting's rich details, bright colors, and bustling atmosphere add a sense of grandeur and collective celebration, enriching the theme with a portrayal of communal love.

3. The Coronation of Napoleon by Jacques-Louis David:

- Continue to **The Coronation of Napoleon** by **Jacques-Louis David**, where the intersection of **love, power, and authority** is on full display. In this monumental painting, Napoleon crowns himself Emperor, while his wife Josephine kneels before him in a symbolic gesture of loyalty and love. This piece explores the idea of love intertwined with ambition, showcasing the personal and political dynamics within one of history's most powerful couples. The blend of love and grandeur adds a layer of complexity to the tour's theme.

4. Gabrielle d'Estrées and One of Her Sisters:

- Conclude the tour with the mysterious and intimate **Gabrielle d'Estrées and One of Her Sisters**. This painting invites reflection on the themes of **love, intimacy, and secrecy**, depicting two women in a private, enigmatic moment. The gesture of one sister pinching Gabrielle's nipple is rich with symbolism, interpreted as a reference to Gabrielle's pregnancy with the future king's child. The painting leaves visitors pondering the subtleties of love—both public and private, open and concealed.

CHAPTER 11: PRACTICAL INFORMATION

Opening Hours and Admission

A visit to the Louvre requires some planning to ensure you get the most out of your experience. Here's everything you need to know about the museum's hours, admission fees, and tips for a smooth visit:

1. Standard Opening Hours:

- The Louvre is open from **9:00 AM to 6:00 PM** every day except Tuesdays. On **Wednesdays and Fridays**, the museum offers extended hours until **9:45 PM**, providing a more relaxed experience with fewer crowds. These late-night openings allow visitors to explore the museum in a quieter, more intimate setting.

2. Admission Fees:

- Standard admission is **€17** when purchased online and **€15** at the museum.

There are **reduced rates** for students, seniors, and **free entry** for EU citizens under 26. Additionally, the Louvre offers **free admission** on the first Sunday of each month, though these days tend to be busier.

3. Purchase Tickets Online:

- To save time and avoid long queues, it's recommended to purchase tickets online in advance, especially during peak tourist seasons. This guarantees your entry and lets you start exploring right away.

4. Special Exhibitions and Guided Tours:

- Special exhibition tickets may come with an additional fee, and guided tours can be booked for those seeking a more curated experience. Prices for guided tours vary but typically range between **€15-€30**, depending on the tour's focus and duration.

Visitor Services

To make your visit comfortable, the Louvre provides a range of visitor services:

1. Amenities:

- The museum offers **restrooms**, **cloakrooms**, and **baby-changing facilities** throughout the galleries, ensuring essential services are readily available. These amenities are clearly marked on museum maps.

2. Audio Guides and Museum Apps:

- Enhance your visit with **audio guides** or the Louvre's **museum app**, which provides in-depth information about the artworks and curated tour options. Audio guides are available for rent at the museum, while the app can be downloaded for free.

3. Accessibility Services:

- The Louvre is fully accessible, with **wheelchair rentals**, **accessible entrances**, and specialized tours for visitors with mobility or sensory impairments.

Contact museum staff in advance to arrange any necessary accommodations.

4. Information Desks and Multilingual Staff:

- Information desks are located near entrances, and **multilingual staff** are available to assist with questions, directions, or general advice throughout the museum, ensuring a hassle-free visit.

Safety and Security

Ensuring a safe and secure visit to the Louvre is a top priority for both visitors and staff. Here's what you can expect in terms of security measures and how to stay safe during your visit:

1. Security Screening Process:

- Upon entering the Louvre, all visitors must go through a **security screening**. This includes **bag checks** and passing through metal detectors. **Large luggage, backpacks, and suitcases** are prohibited inside the museum, so it's best to leave bulky items at your hotel or in storage.

There are lockers available for smaller bags and personal items, but it's important to keep your belongings compact and manageable to ensure a smooth entry.

2. Safeguarding Personal Belongings:

- The Louvre is a popular and often crowded attraction, making it important to stay vigilant about your **personal belongings**. Keep wallets, phones, and other valuables close to your body, preferably in a zipped bag or money belt. Be especially cautious in crowded areas, such as near the **Mona Lisa** or **Venus de Milo**, where pickpocketing can occur. Always be mindful of your surroundings and avoid leaving your belongings unattended.

3. Emergency Contact Numbers and First Aid:

- The Louvre has **first-aid services** available should you need assistance during your visit. In case of an emergency, contact Louvre staff or security, or dial the Louvre Museum's **emergency number**: +33 (0)1 40 20 53 17.

Staff are trained to handle emergencies and can provide medical assistance or direct you to the nearest first-aid station.

4. French Emergency Contact Information:

- For emergencies outside the museum, here are the key numbers to know:

    o **Police and Emergency Services**: Dial **112** (universal European emergency number) or **17** for police.

    o **Medical Emergencies**: Dial **15** for **SAMU** (French medical emergency services).

    o **Fire Department**: Dial **18** for the **Pompiers** (fire and medical emergencies).

    o **Lost and Found (Louvre)**: +33 (0)1 40 20 53 17.

    o **Nearest Hospital**: **Hôpital Cochin** (27 Rue du Faubourg Saint-Jacques, 75014 Paris) | Phone: +33 (0)1 58 41 41 41.

Helpful Tips for a Stress-Free Visit

Here are some practical tips to make your Louvre visit as smooth and enjoyable as possible:

1. Dress Comfortably:

- The Louvre is vast and involves a lot of walking. Wear **comfortable shoes** and dress in layers to stay comfortable throughout the day.

2. Bring Snacks and Water:

- While there are cafés on-site, they can be pricey. Consider bringing your own **snacks and water** to stay energized and hydrated during your visit.

3. Museum Maps:

- Download the **Louvre map** in advance or pick one up at the entrance. This will help you navigate the museum and ensure you don't miss any of your must-see works.

4. Take Breaks:

- To avoid burnout, take breaks in quieter galleries or outdoor spaces like the **Cour Marly** or **Cour Puget**, which offer peaceful spots to rest and reflect on the art.

Language Tips and Phrases for Visiting the Louvre

Navigating the Louvre and Paris as a non-French speaker can be easier with a few helpful phrases. Here are some key **French phrases** and **tips** to make your visit smoother, especially when interacting with museum staff or getting around Paris.

Basic Greetings and Courtesies:

- **Bonjour** (bohn-zhoor) – Hello / Good day

- **Bonsoir** (bohn-swahr) – Good evening

- **Merci** (mehr-see) – Thank you

- **S'il vous plaît** (seel voo pleh) – Please

- **Excusez-moi** (ehk-skew-zay mwah) – Excuse me

- **Au revoir** (oh ruh-vwahr) – Goodbye

Asking for Directions or Information:

- **Où se trouve... ?** (oo suh troov...) – Where is...?

- **Les toilettes, s'il vous plaît ?** (lay twah-let, seel voo pleh?) – Where are the restrooms, please?

- **Comment aller à... ?** (koh-mohn ah-lay ah...?) – How do I get to…?

- **Pouvez-vous m'aider ?** (poo-vay voo may-day?) – Can you help me?

At the Museum:

- **Un billet, s'il vous plaît.** (uhn bee-yay, seel voo pleh) – One ticket, please.

- **Y a-t-il une visite guidée ?** (ee-ah teel oon vee-zeet gee-day?) – Is there a guided tour?

- **Est-ce qu'il y a des audioguides ?** (ehs keel ee ah day oh-dee-oh-geed?) – Are there audio guides?

- **À quelle heure ferme le musée ?** (ah kehl uhr fehrm luh mew-zay?) – What time does the museum close?

In a Café or Restaurant:

- **La carte, s'il vous plaît.** (lah kart, seel voo pleh) – The menu, please.

- **Je voudrais...** (zhuh voo-dray...) – I would like...

- **L'addition, s'il vous plaît.** (lah-dee-syon, seel voo pleh) – The bill, please.

Directions and Transport:

- **Où est la station de métro ?** (oo ay lah stah-syon duh may-troh?) – Where is the metro station?

- **Un billet pour le métro, s'il vous plaît.** (uhn bee-yay poor luh may-troh, seel voo pleh) – One metro ticket, please.

- **C'est à quelle distance ?** (seh ah kehl dee-stahns?) – How far is it?

Emergency Phrases:

- **Appelez une ambulance !** (ah-peh-lay oon ahm-bew-lahnss!) – Call an ambulance!

- **J'ai besoin d'aide.** (zhay buh-zwan dehd) – I need help.

- **Où est l'hôpital ?** (oo ay loh-pee-tal?) – Where is the hospital?

Tips for Language Interaction:

- **Politeness goes a long way**: Always start with "Bonjour" or "Bonsoir" when addressing someone.

- **Speak slowly**: If your French is limited, it's helpful to speak slowly. Many Parisians can understand basic English but appreciate an effort to speak French.

- **Use simple phrases**: Even if you're unsure, attempting a few basic phrases shows respect and will likely result in a friendly response.

Chapter 12: Essential Travel Checklist

1. Important Documents:

Passport: Ensure your passport is valid for at least six months beyond your travel dates.

- **Travel Insurance**: Print and carry a copy of your insurance policy and emergency contact numbers.

- **Flight Tickets**: Keep a digital and printed copy of your e-tickets or boarding passes.

- **Hotel Reservations**: Have a confirmation of your booking, including the hotel's address and contact details.

- **Louvre Tickets**: Purchase tickets online in advance and carry a digital or printed copy to avoid long lines.

- **Transportation Passes**: Consider purchasing a Paris Metro pass or museum pass for convenience.

2. Health and Safety Essentials:

- **Vaccination Records**: If required, carry proof of vaccination or any necessary health documents.

- **Medications**: Pack a sufficient supply of any prescription medications, along with a copy of the prescription.

- **Face Mask & Sanitizer**: Bring face masks and hand sanitizer for public spaces and crowded areas.

- **First-Aid Kit**: Include band-aids, pain relievers, motion sickness tablets, and any personal health items.

3. Tech and Gadgets:

- **Smartphone**: Load useful apps like Google Maps, language translation tools, and the Louvre's official app for audio guides.

- **Camera/Phone Charger**: Make sure you have chargers for your phone and any electronic devices.

- **Power Adapter**: Bring a universal power adapter for charging devices in France (Type C and Type E sockets).

- **Portable Battery**: A backup power bank can be useful for long days exploring the city.

4. Personal Comfort Items:

- **Comfortable Shoes**: You'll be walking a lot, so pack well-cushioned shoes for exploring the Louvre and Paris.

- **Weather-Appropriate Clothing**: Check the forecast before packing. If visiting in winter, bring warm layers, and for summer, light clothing and sunscreen.

- **Reusable Water Bottle**: Many museums, including the Louvre, allow water bottles, so stay hydrated during your visit.

- **Umbrella**: Paris weather can be unpredictable, so pack a small travel umbrella just in case.

5. Money and Financials:

- **Credit/Debit Cards**: Carry cards with international capability and notify your bank of travel plans.

- **Cash**: It's useful to have euros on hand for smaller purchases or tips.

- **Currency Converter App**: Use an app to quickly convert prices when shopping or dining.

6. Navigational Tools:

- **Maps and Guidebooks**: Carry a small guidebook or download an offline map of Paris in case of poor mobile signal.

- **Louvre Museum Map**: Download or pick up a map at the entrance to plan your visit effectively.

- **Itinerary**: Have a rough itinerary for your days in Paris, including key spots you want to visit beyond the Louvre.

7. Packing for a Day at the Louvre:

- **Small Backpack or Bag**: Use a compact bag for essentials like your phone, wallet, and water bottle. Remember, large bags aren't allowed inside the museum.

- **Snacks**: Pack light, non-messy snacks if you need a quick bite during your museum visit.

- **Notebook & Pen**: If you enjoy taking notes about the art or your experiences, bring a small notebook.

FINAL THOUGHTS

As you step away from the Louvre's iconic glass pyramid and reflect on your journey through one of the world's greatest cultural treasures, it's clear that the experience has left an indelible mark. Visiting the Louvre is not just about seeing famous artworks—it's about connecting with the artists, the stories, and the history that have shaped our world. Each brushstroke, each sculpture, each ancient artifact offers a glimpse into the human experience, spanning centuries of creativity, emotion, and vision.

Walking through the Louvre, you've stood in front of masterpieces that have captivated the world—**Mona Lisa's** mysterious smile, the commanding presence of the **Winged Victory of Samothrace**, the ethereal beauty of the **Venus de Milo**. But beyond the well-known highlights, you've also ventured into quieter corners, perhaps discovering hidden gems in the **Islamic Art** section, marveling at the intricate craftsmanship of the **Decorative Arts**, or losing yourself in the serene beauty of the **Cour Marly**.

This is the magic of the Louvre. It's a place where time stands still, where you can connect with art in a deeply personal way. It's a place that reminds us of the power of human creativity—how a single painting or sculpture can evoke emotions, provoke thought, and inspire generations.

But as compelling as the Louvre is, it's just the beginning. This journey through art and history doesn't end here. **Your curiosity has been sparked**—now, what will you do with it? The world is full of treasures waiting to be explored, stories waiting to be heard, and experiences that will broaden your perspective even further.

Take a moment to consider what you've learned, what's moved you, and how this experience has opened your eyes to the beauty and complexity of the world. Whether you choose to dive deeper into art history, explore more museums, or embark on new travels, let this be the starting point of a lifelong journey of discovery.

Here's your call to action: Don't stop with the Louvre. Use this experience as a springboard to fuel your curiosity. Whether you're a seasoned traveler or someone who's just starting to explore, let the awe and wonder you felt at the

Louvre guide you to new adventures. There are countless museums, galleries, and cultural landmarks waiting for you, each offering its own unique insight into the human spirit.

Visit the **Musée d'Orsay** and immerse yourself in the vibrant world of the Impressionists. Walk through **Giverny**, where **Monet's Water Lilies** come to life. Explore the streets of **Montmartre**, where creativity still hums in the air. Or venture further, beyond Paris, into the vast and varied cultural landscapes of the world—places where art and history continue to shape our collective story.

And while you're at it, **share your experiences**. Tell others about the emotions you felt standing in front of **Liberty Leading the People**, or the way the quiet corners of the Louvre made you reflect on your own life and history. Inspire others to see the world through a new lens—one that's informed by the art, culture, and history you've encountered.

The world is vast, and its beauty is endless. You've taken the first step by exploring the Louvre—now, it's time to keep going. Seek out new stories, discover new places, and continue to let art shape the way you see the world. **The journey is yours to create**.

What will you discover next?

Your adventure doesn't end here. **Go find your next masterpiece.**

I hope this book has been a valuable and enjoyable resource for you. If you found it helpful or inspiring, I would truly appreciate it if you could rate it 5 stars and leave a glowing review. Your support means the world and helps others find and enjoy the book too. Thank you so much!

LOUVRE MUSEUM

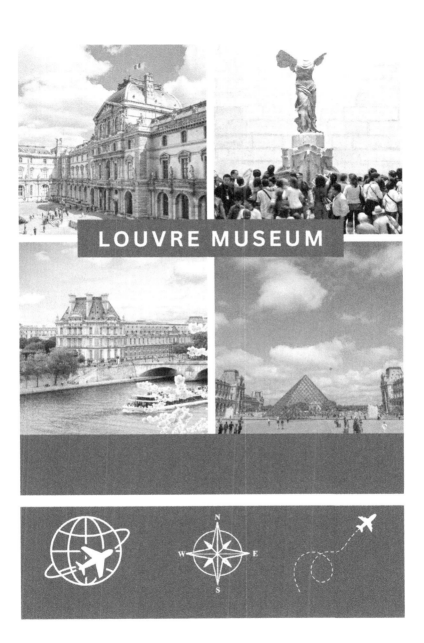

LOUVRE MUSEUM

Made in the USA
Las Vegas, NV
31 May 2025

22908921R10079